On the Job

FIRST RESPONDERS

Expressions, Equations, and Inequalities

Vickie An

Contributing Author

Alison S. Marzocchi, Ph.D.

Consultant

Colleen Pollitt, M.A.Ed.
Math Support Teacher
Howard County Public Schools

Publishing Credits

Rachelle Cracchiolo, M.S.Ed., *Publisher*
Conni Medina, M.A.Ed., *Editor in Chief*
Dona Herweck Rice, *Series Developer*
Emily R. Smith, M.A.Ed., *Series Developer*
Diana Kenney, M.A.Ed., NBCT, *Content Director*
Stacy Monsman, M.A., *Editor*
Michelle Jovin, M.A., *Associate Editor*
Fabiola Sepulveda, *Graphic Designer*

Image Credits: p.6 (top) Douglas Graham/Loudoun Now/Newscom; p.14 My Life Graphic/Shutterstock; p.15 (bottom) Jeff Thrower/Shutterstock; p.16 (left) Boris Roessler/dpa/Newscom; p.16 (right) Reuters/Newscom; p.17 DanitaDelimont/Newscom; p18 (top) cdsb-Imaginechina/Newscom; p.18 (bottom) Ratib Al Safadi/Anadolu Agency/Getty Images; p.19 Rafael Ben Ari/Chameleons Eye/Newscom; p.20 Yuriko Nakao/Reuters/Newscom; p.21 Kyodo News via Getty Images; p.23 (top) UPI/Newscom; p.23 (bottom) Polaris/Newscom; p.24 (left) Josiah Dewey/Zuma Press/Newscom; p.25 Ed Zurga/Reuters/Newscom; pp.26–27 Peter O'Toole/iStock; all other images from iStock and/or Shutterstock.

Library of Congress Cataloging-in-Publication Data

Names: An, Vickie, author.
Title: First responders : expressions, equations, and inequalities / Vickie An.
Description: Huntington Beach, CA : Teacher Created Materials, [2019] | Series: On the job | Audience: Grades 4 to 6. | Includes index. | Identifiers: LCCN 2018051875 (print) | LCCN 2018052915 (ebook) | ISBN 9781425855307 (eBook) | ISBN 9781425858865 (pbk. : alk. paper)
Subjects: LCSH: First responders--Juvenile literature. | Emergency management--Juvenile literature. | Mathematics--Juvenile literature.
Classification: LCC HV554.3 (ebook) | LCC HV554.3 .A5 2019 (print) | DDC 362.18--dc23
LC record available at https://lccn.loc.gov/2018051875

Teacher Created Materials
5301 Oceanus Drive
Huntington Beach, CA 92649-1030
www.tcmpub.com

ISBN 978-1-4258-5886-5

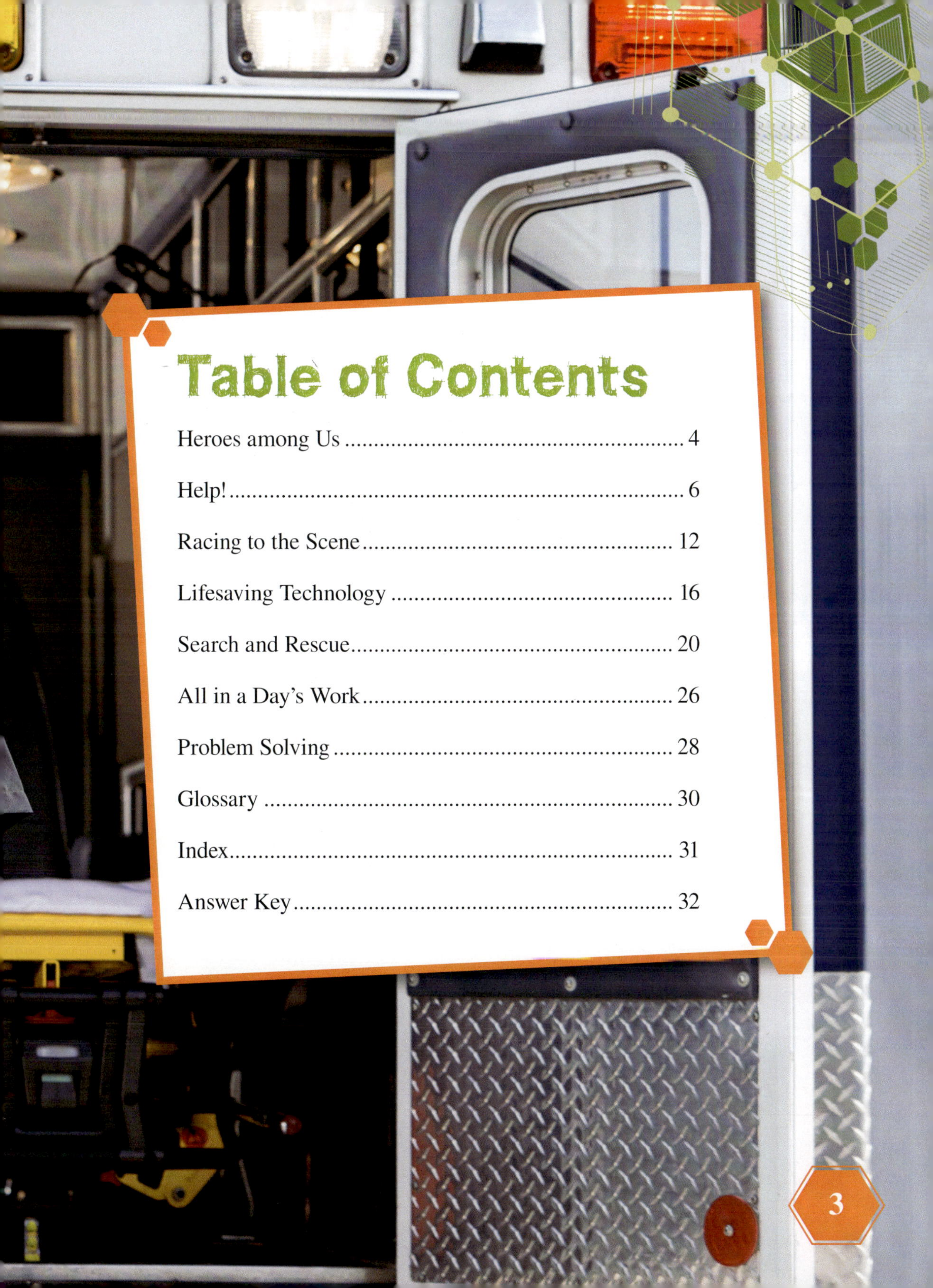

Table of Contents

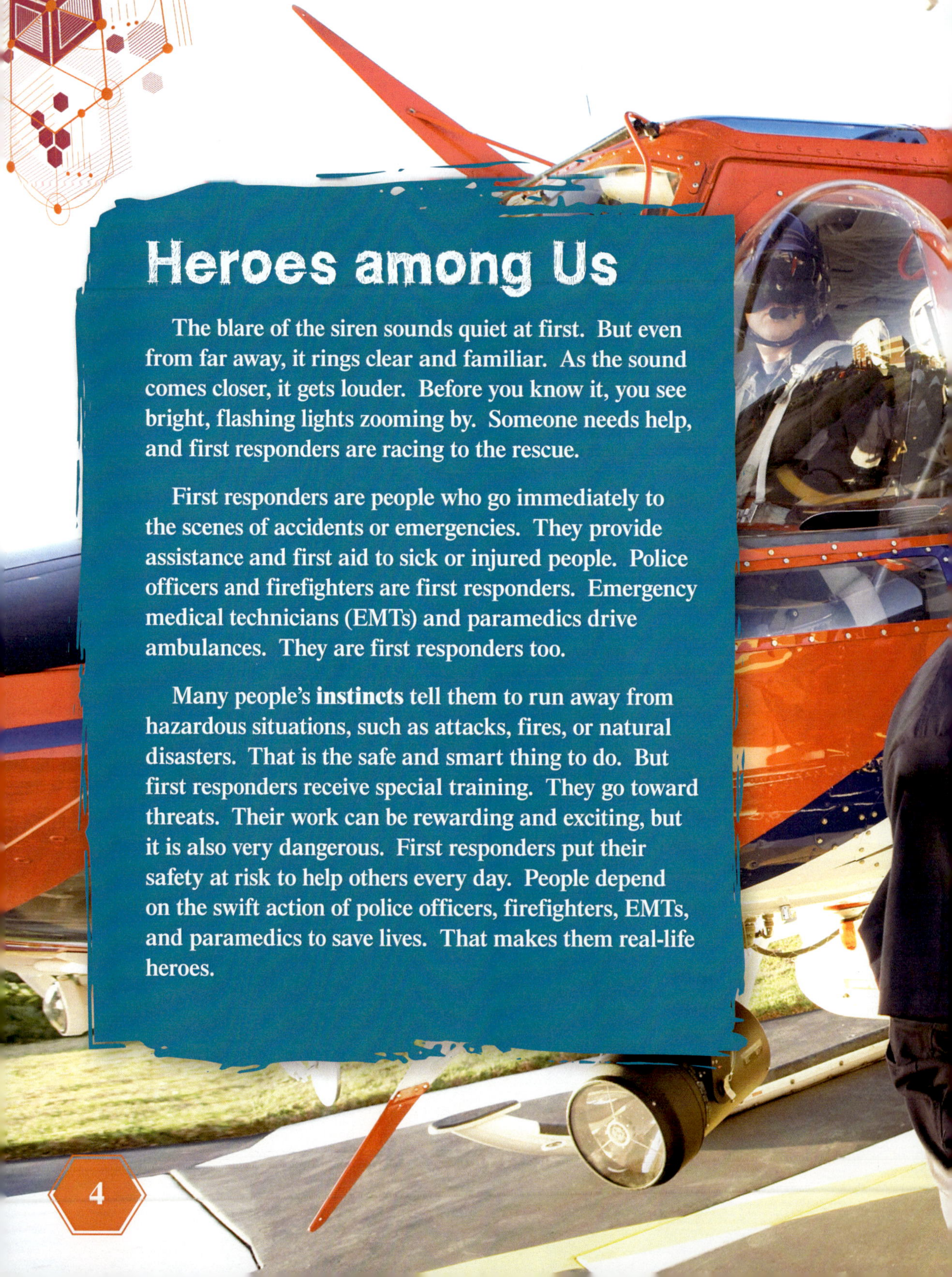

Heroes among Us

The blare of the siren sounds quiet at first. But even from far away, it rings clear and familiar. As the sound comes closer, it gets louder. Before you know it, you see bright, flashing lights zooming by. Someone needs help, and first responders are racing to the rescue.

First responders are people who go immediately to the scenes of accidents or emergencies. They provide assistance and first aid to sick or injured people. Police officers and firefighters are first responders. Emergency medical technicians (EMTs) and paramedics drive ambulances. They are first responders too.

Many people's **instincts** tell them to run away from hazardous situations, such as attacks, fires, or natural disasters. That is the safe and smart thing to do. But first responders receive special training. They go toward threats. Their work can be rewarding and exciting, but it is also very dangerous. First responders put their safety at risk to help others every day. People depend on the swift action of police officers, firefighters, EMTs, and paramedics to save lives. That makes them real-life heroes.

Help!

First responders usually arrive at the scene of an accident or **crisis** within minutes of being alerted by a **dispatcher**. People who phone for help often reach emergency dispatchers first. Dispatchers work at call centers, police stations, and fire stations. They have to think fast. They must keep callers calm while gathering information so they know who to send for help. Many dispatchers have emergency medical training. This helps them guide callers on how to give aid until help arrives.

A dispatcher works at a call center.

Usually, the police respond to reports of a crime or accident. Firefighters battle blazes and inspect gas leaks. They conduct rescues during natural disasters as well. EMTs and paramedics rush in if someone needs medical attention. Police officers and firefighters are trained in basic first aid too. Sometimes, police officers, firefighters, EMTs, and paramedics will all show up to a scene together.

Trained for Traumas

On arrival, emergency responders quickly evaluate the situation. Is there still danger? Who's hurt? Do others need to be led to safety? Is the road clear for emergency vehicles to pass? When the scene is secure, they work to help victims.

Many times, first responders perform first aid on the spot. First aid is care given to a sick or injured person before advanced medical treatment can be obtained. It's meant to prevent the person's injury or illness from getting worse.

Paramedics perform first aid on an injured man.

LET'S EXPLORE MATH

Imagine that dispatchers write expressions to record how many emergency calls they receive each hour for four hours.

Dispatcher A: 4×4

Dispatcher B: 4^2

Dispatcher C: $4 + 4 + 4 + 4$

Draw diagrams to prove whether the dispatchers received the same number of calls.

People perform first aid every day. Have you ever had a deep cut that needed stitches? If so, a parent, teacher, or another adult probably used a clean towel to apply pressure on the wound or bandaged it before rushing you to the doctor. This not only helps stop the bleeding, but it also keeps bacteria out of the cut so it doesn't get infected.

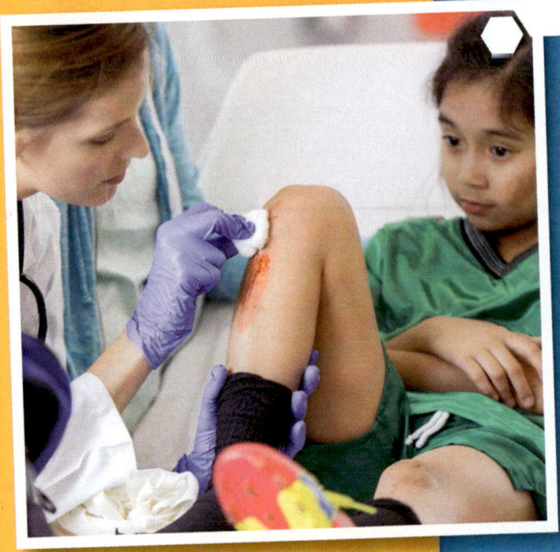

That's just one example of first aid. Some injuries are far more serious. In those cases, being trained in first aid can determine the difference between life and death.

How to Save a Life

In any situation, emergency responders want to **stabilize** victims as soon as possible. They **evaluate** patients' needs in a number of ways. Two big things responders check for are if people suffered any injuries and if they are having trouble breathing. Responders might measure heart rate and blood pressure and examine skin too. Do the patients look pale? Are they burning up or freezing cold? Are their hearts beating faster than normal? The answers to these questions and more provide critical clues for the type of care the patients need.

First responders are also trained in **cardiopulmonary resuscitation** (kar-dee-oh-PUL-muh-nare-ee rih-suh-suh-TAY-shun), or CPR. *Cardio* means "heart." *Pulmonary* means "of the lungs." To *resuscitate* means "to bring someone back to life."

Emergency responders perform CPR on an injured woman.

LET'S EXPLORE MATH

A normal resting heart rate for an adult is between 60 and 100 beats per minute. Carla counts her heartbeats while finding her pulse for 20 seconds, or $\frac{1}{3}$ of a minute. She writes two inequalities, where b represents the number of beats she counts in 20 seconds.

$$3b \geq 60 \qquad 3b \leq 100$$

1. Why is b multiplied by 3 in each inequality?

Use the set of possible heartbeat counts **{18, 20, 31, 36}** to answer questions 2 and 3.

2. Which heartbeat counts from the set would make both inequalities true, representing healthy heart rates?
3. Which heartbeat counts from the set would make one inequality true but not the other, representing unhealthy heart rates?

CPR is a lifesaving technique used when people stop breathing or their hearts stop beating. This can happen during a heart attack, a near drowning, choking, or other medical emergency. Anyone, not just first responders and medical professionals, can learn CPR. The lifeguards at local pools know CPR. Teachers, coaches, and babysitters may know CPR as well. Ask your adult family members if they have been trained. You can take a class to learn CPR too. After all, you never know when someone may need help.

Sometimes, to restart the heart, rescuers use a machine called an automated external defibrillator (dee-fih-BRUH-lay-tuhr), or an AED. This is a portable device that delivers an electric shock through the chest to the heart. Shocking the heart can potentially get it beating again.

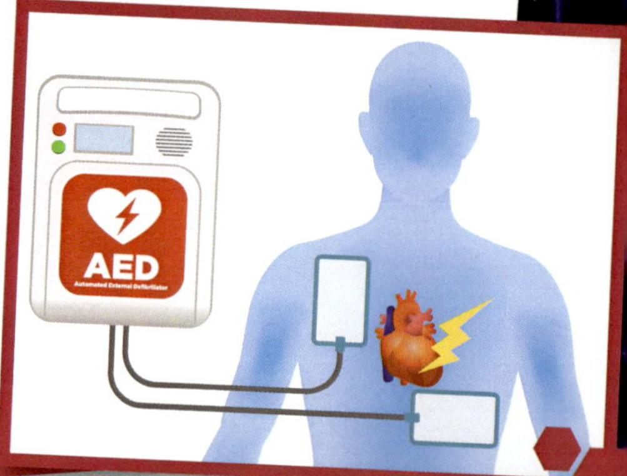

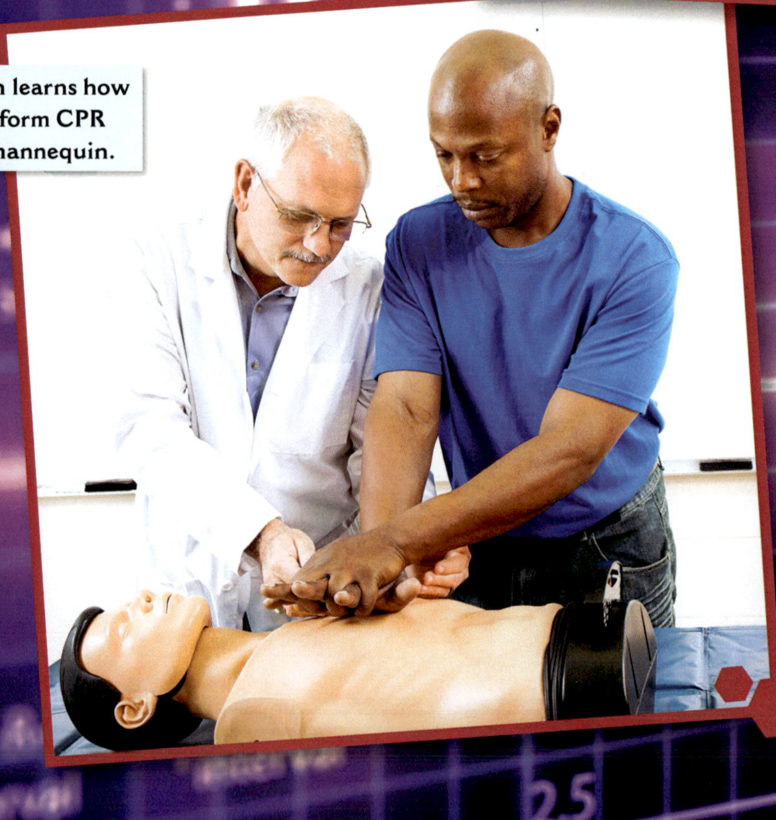

A man learns how to perform CPR on a mannequin.

Many people panic in an emergency. Like dispatchers, first responders try to help people stay calm. So communication is key. One thing first responders might do to ease fear is to look their patients in the eye and give them encouragement. They may also describe what they are doing as they provide care. These and other practices can help people stay calm during a crisis.

LET'S EXPLORE MATH

Lifeguards trained in CPR alternate between 2 rescue breaths and 30 chest compressions. They repeat this pattern until first responders arrive. Use r to represent the number of rounds of CPR. Choose all the expressions that can be used to calculate the total number of chest compressions.

A. $30r$

B. $r(20 + 10)$

C. $30 + 30 + 30$

D. $r \times 30$

E. $15r + 15r$

F. 30^r

Racing to the Scene

Before they can help anyone, first responders must be able to travel to the scene of a crisis or to the hospital safely and swiftly. Remember those loud sirens and flashing lights? Without them, emergency vehicles would have a hard time warning drivers they need to pass.

Official emergency vehicles include police cars, fire trucks, and ambulances. Sometimes, police officers ride motorcycles, bicycles, or even horses. Colors of emergency lights can differ by city, state, and country. Most places use red or blue or a combination of both. Some people say a mix of red and blue makes the most sense. Why? One common argument is that red is easier to see during the day, and blue is easier to see at night. Some studies **dispute** this and say that blue lights are more visible at any time.

There are a few different types of sirens on the road when emergency vehicles need to get through. The wail is probably the most famous. It creates a high-pitched, long howl that rises and falls. You may also recognize the yelp, which has a sharp, rapidly changing pitch. The phaser sounds similar to a laser tag gun. And then there's the "hi-lo" siren, which alternates between two tones. Emergency responders may choose to use different sirens to try to get drivers' attention.

LET'S EXPLORE MATH

Imagine that a fire department tracks response times. It takes firefighters 2 minutes to put on their gear and load the truck. It takes an average of $1\frac{1}{2}$ minutes per mile to drive to the scene. They want to find out how far they can travel to have response times of 20 minutes or less. The chief writes this inequality:

$$\mathbf{2 + 1\tfrac{1}{2}\boldsymbol{m} \leq 20}$$

1. What does the *m* represent in the inequality? What does the 2 represent? Why did the chief use $\leq$ instead of $<$?

Use the set of possible distances **{8 miles, 12 miles, 14 miles}** to answer question 2.

2. Which distances from the set allow the fire department to arrive in 20 minutes or less?

In any case, when drivers hear the sirens or see the lights of a police cruiser, fire engine, or ambulance approaching, it's a sign. They need to pull over to the side of the road and stop. Every minute counts in an emergency!

What's on Board?

Emergency vehicles are equipped with gear that helps first responders do their jobs. For example, ambulances have medical equipment to treat patients at the scenes and on the way to the hospitals. This includes medicine and bandages. There are also **splints** for broken bones, neck braces to keep someone's head still, and stretchers to move patients safely. Ambulances also have machines that monitor **vital signs**. They track temperature, heart rate, breathing rate, and blood pressure.

Police cars and fire trucks also carry basic medical supplies, such as first-aid kits and AEDs. Police officers might also keep body armor and other tools that they need at crime scenes in the trunks of their cars. And fire engines might also carry tools, hoses, ladders, and even equipment to get into damaged vehicles.

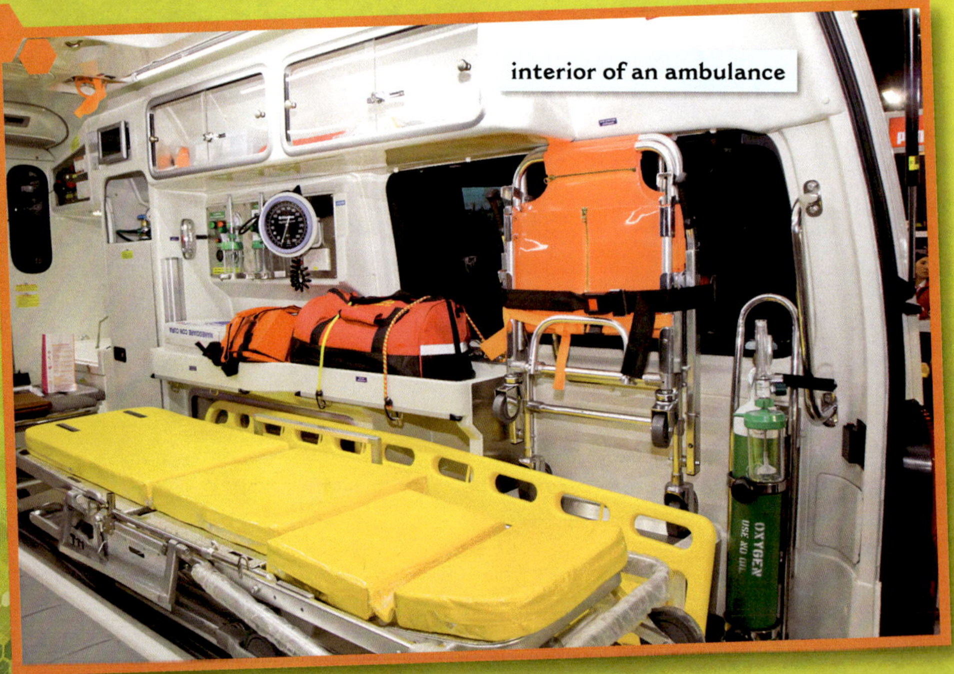

interior of an ambulance

interior of a rescue helicopter

A firefighter uses a tool to pry open a van door.

Lifesaving Technology

Today, first responders are adding high-tech gear to their tools. These advancements allow rescuers to see more. And that means they can help more people.

Have you ever seen a camera drone in the sky? These flying robots have experienced a recent **surge** in popularity. People use them to take pictures and videos from high in the air. Camera drones are usually connected to an app. This allows the people controlling them to see views from above. Because drones capture **aerial** images, first responders use them in rescue missions.

How can this technology help save lives? It gives first responders a better understanding of the problems they're facing. For instance, a police officer might use a drone to see where a dangerous suspect could be hiding. This keeps officers safe and helps them catch the suspect.

In another situation, firefighters might send a drone with **thermal imaging cameras** into a burning building. These cameras sense heat given off by people or objects. This can help firefighters find victims through heavy smoke. The drone can also point out hot spots to stay away from or flames to put out.

First responders study aerial drone footage after an earthquake.

A firefighter uses a thermal imaging camera to search inside a burning building.

Drones can be used for more than just eyes in the sky. They can also deliver lifesaving supplies to people who need help but cannot be reached right away. For instance, drones can drop drinking water, food, medicine, or life jackets to people trapped by natural disasters. Or they can search for people who are lost. These small, unmanned aircraft have saved numerous lives around the world.

A drone delivers medicine to people who live in a remote area of China.

Emergency responders use a drone to search for and rescue people in danger of drowning.

Get Smart

Smartphones can also help save people during emergencies. Some local emergency response officials have created special apps that send lifesaving information to communities. These apps give people important updates in real time. This can include things such as the location of shelters during hurricanes or flooded streets to avoid. The apps can tell where wildfires have spread. Or they can track and predict paths of tornadoes.

Many people use social media to get their news as well. First responders can use tools such as Facebook® and Twitter™ to get critical information to people.

Engineers and scientists are hard at work creating more technology that will help first responders tackle **perilous** situations. There are remote-controlled machines that can remove rubble and search for victims. There are robots that act as water cannons. All these inventions aim to keep first responders out of harm's way as they save lives.

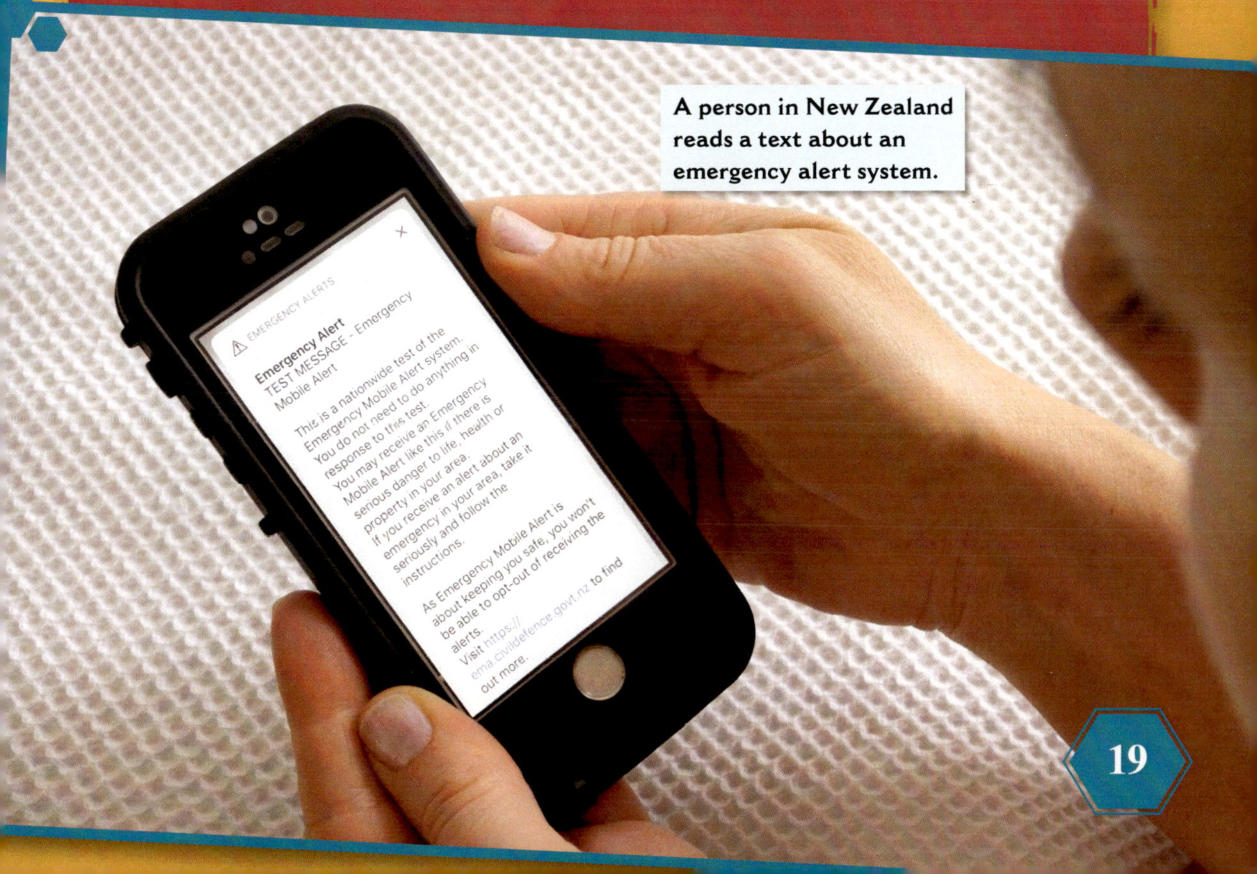

A person in New Zealand reads a text about an emergency alert system.

Search and Rescue

First responders are called to help in disasters around the world. Some situations are more dangerous than others. In natural disasters, complications often arise that can make things even more **treacherous** for first responders.

Earthquake in Japan

On March 11, 2011, a 9.0 earthquake struck near Tokyo. It was the largest earthquake to ever hit Japan. The strength of the earthquake triggered a tsunami that hit the coast soon after. The two events caused a major problem on Japan's island of Honshu. A nuclear power plant was damaged and left without power. Radiation leaked, followed by explosions due to system failures.

First responders had their work cut out for them. After the tsunami, they searched for survivors in the wreckage left behind. At the same time, people who lived near the nuclear power plant had to be evacuated. Teams from around the world flew in to help find survivors. They rescued some people from their homes. They even saved one man floating on the roof of his house. As aftershocks continued for days after the initial earthquake, rescue teams didn't give up.

First responders wash a man whom they rescued from the damaged nuclear power plant in Japan.

An emergency responder walks by houses that were leveled by the 2011 earthquake.

LET'S EXPLORE MATH

Imagine that a team of first responders evacuates survivors during an emergency. On average, they evacuate 15 people per hour. So far, they have evacuated 195 people.

1. Use h to represent the number of hours the team has been working. Write an equation to represent the situation.
2. A news reporter asks if he can tell viewers that the team has been evacuating people for 24 hours. Is this accurate? Why or why not?
3. How many hours has the team been evacuating people? Use your equation to prove your solution.

Hurricane Season

In August 2017, Hurricane Harvey slammed into the Texas coast. More than 40 inches (102 centimeters) of rain poured down in the Houston area. The storm caused severe flooding all over the city. Many families were trapped by rapidly rising floodwaters in their homes and needed rescue. As always, first responders sprang into action.

Rescuers set out in rafts and boats. They used drones to locate areas that needed the most help. They searched flooded neighborhoods for stranded homeowners and got them to shelters. They waded through the streets, carrying people to safety in their arms. High winds, fast-moving water, and **debris** made conditions scary. First responders had their own families to worry about too. But they kept going, saving thousands of people.

This was just the beginning of hurricane season for that year. Days after Harvey, Hurricane Irma hit the Caribbean islands and Florida. Hurricane Maria drenched Puerto Rico soon after. Then, a few weeks later, Hurricane Nate struck the Gulf Coast. The storm came only 12 years after Hurricane Katrina destroyed the region in 2005. With every storm that came, first responders got to work.

LET'S EXPLORE MATH

Imagine that a charitable organization raises money, so it can donate $1,500 to each family affected by a hurricane. It will donate an additional $14,000 to help with repairs. So far, it has raised a total of $320,000. The treasurer of the charity uses f to represent the number of families and writes this equation:

$$1{,}500f + 14{,}000 = 320{,}000$$

1. After the donation to the city, can the organization help 24, 204, or 2,004 families? Use the equation to prove your choice.
2. How much money does the organization need to raise if it wants to help 500 families and still donate $14,000 to the city?

Texas National Guard soldiers help people in Houston after Hurricane Harvey.

A first responder rescues a child after Hurricane Florence hit parts of the East Coast in 2018.

Fighting Fires

In July 2018, a series of wildfires broke out in Northern California. At the height of the firestorm, more than 14,000 firefighters fought the blazes. The firefighters came from other states and around the world. Along with fire engines, crews used helicopters and air tankers to combat the spreading fires. Firefighters worked night and day to put out the fires. They also helped evacuate thousands of residents and save as many structures as they could. By the time the fires were put out, they had become the largest series of wildfires in the state's history.

Firefighters work to extinguish a wildfire in Sonora, California, in August 2018.

Terrible Tornado

On May 22, 2011, a tornado touched down in Joplin, Missouri. It was on the ground for 38 minutes with wind speeds over 200 miles (322 kilometers) per hour. Gas leaks and downed wires made relief and rescue efforts difficult. Hundreds of firefighters, police officers, and others rushed to help less than 12 hours after the tornado hit. Many of them had lost their own homes but were digging through debris to find survivors. Two first responders were struck by lightning while helping with the search when severe weather followed the tornado. The dedication of these men and women is to be admired.

First responders search for survivors in Joplin, Missouri.

All in a Day's Work

First responders care deeply about their communities and make a **commitment** to protect and serve others. People count on their assistance during all kinds of crises, from car accidents and medical emergencies to wildfires and floods.

It is by no means an easy job and can be quite **harrowing** at times. Remember, while they are **bona fide** heroes, they do not possess superpowers. The brave men and women who train and work as first responders are regular people with families of their own. But with every call for help they answer, they willingly put their lives on the line in their sprint toward danger. They do so to keep us, our loved ones, and our neighbors safe. It's all in a day's work for these courageous souls.

So, when you see police officers, firefighters, EMTs, paramedics, or other first responders, don't be shy. Go greet them and shake their hands. That is, if they aren't in the middle of a rescue! Express your gratitude. Give them high fives, and say thank you. They will appreciate it. And the next time you hear the blare of a siren or see those flashing lights, you know that first responders are on their way to help!

Problem Solving

During severe winter storms, conditions are dangerous. Temperatures may be dangerously low. There can be ice and snow on the roads. Emergency personnel may advise residents to stay indoors. When severe storms happen, it is important for residents to be prepared because it can take first responders longer to arrive if help is needed.

Imagine that a volunteer team prepares first aid kits to deliver to homes before any winter storms hit. Use the kit information sheet on page 29 to help plan the preparation and delivery of the kits. Remember to identify what any variables represent.

1. Write the most helpful expressions the team can use to calculate how many total items are needed to make all the kits. Why are your expressions the most helpful?
2. According to a map, at least 140 homes need kits. How many kits do you recommend the team prepare? Why?
3. Use your expressions to calculate how many of each item the team needs to prepare your recommended number of kits.
4. Each volunteer can deliver no more than 12 kits because of how much time it takes to deliver. How many volunteers should you assign to make deliveries? How many kits should you give each of them to deliver? Write an equation to justify your recommendations.
5. A charitable organization's president calls the volunteer team leader and says her group can donate up to 300 canned goods to include in the kits. How many canned goods can you include in each kit if each one must have the same number of items? Write an inequality to show your reasoning.

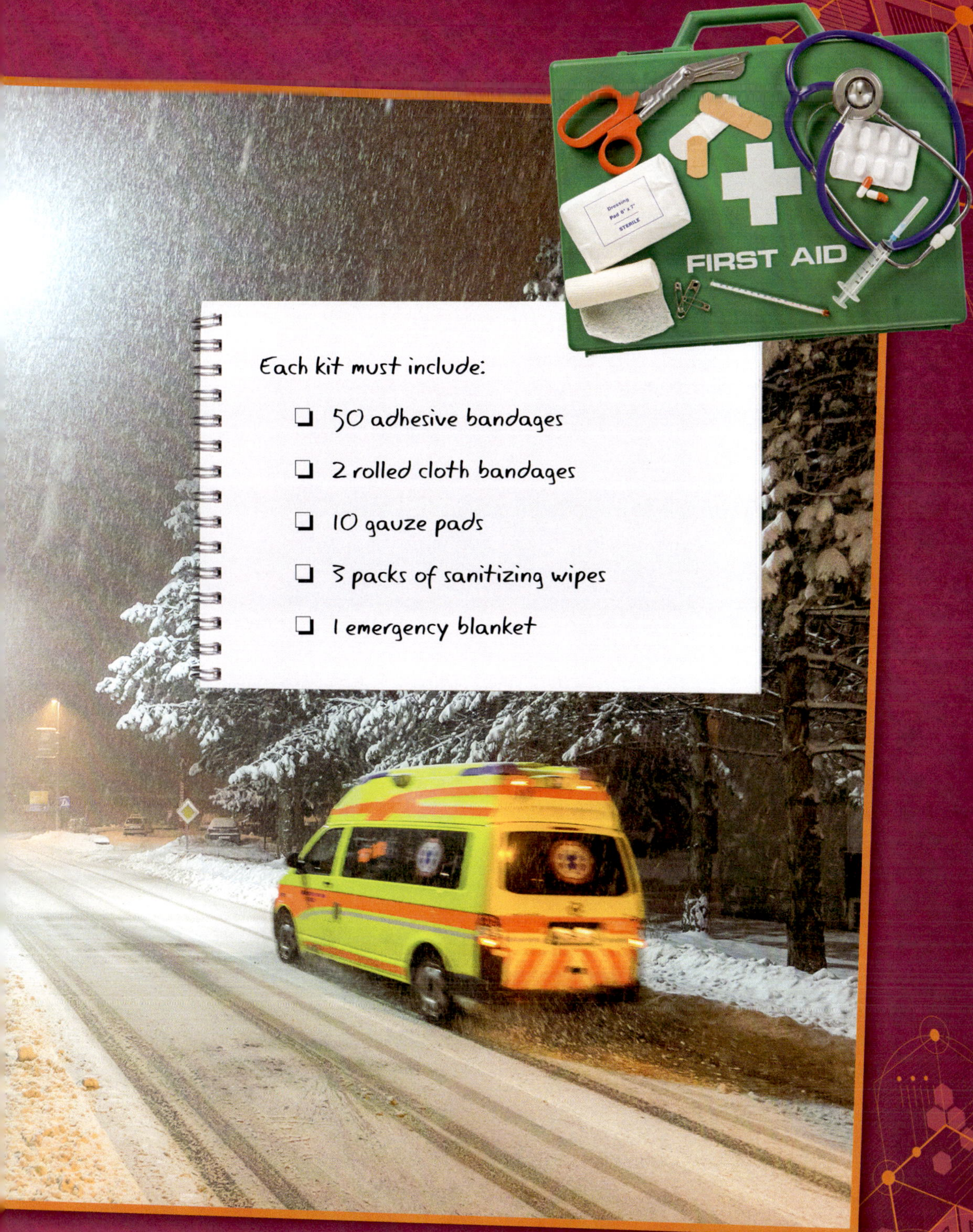

Each kit must include:

- ❏ 50 adhesive bandages
- ❏ 2 rolled cloth bandages
- ❏ 10 gauze pads
- ❏ 3 packs of sanitizing wipes
- ❏ 1 emergency blanket

Glossary

aerial—occurring in the air

bona fide—true or real

cardiopulmonary resuscitation—a procedure also known as CPR, which is used to restore normal breathing when the heart stops beating

commitment—a promise or agreement to do something

crisis—a situation that has become very serious

debris—the remains of something destroyed

dispatcher—communications professional who works with police, firefighters, and EMTs to provide quick responses to emergencies

dispute—to debate or argue

evaluate—to determine the condition of something after study

harrowing—scary

instincts—behaviors that are based on automatic actions

perilous—dangerous or unsafe

splints—devices used to protect body parts and keep them in place

stabilize—to make stable and unlikely to change or decline

surge—a sudden rise

thermal imaging cameras—types of cameras that use the heat given off by objects to produce images of the objects or to locate them

treacherous—very dangerous

vital signs—the measurements of the body's basic functions

Index

Answer Key

Let's Explore Math

page 7

Each dispatcher received 16 calls. Diagrams will vary. Examples:

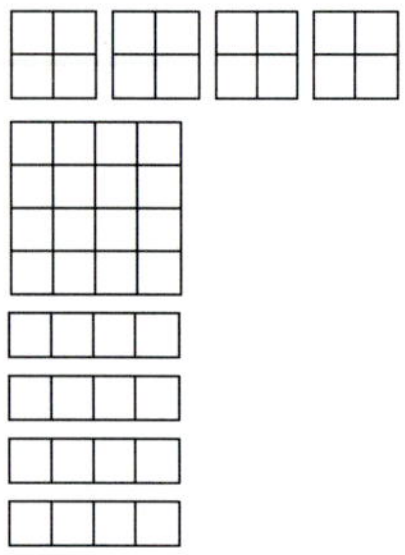

page 9

1. Since *b* represents the number of beats in 20 seconds, or $\frac{1}{3}$ of a minute, it is multiplied by 3 to find out how many beats there are in one minute.
2. 20; 31
3. 18; 36

page 11

A, B, D, E

page 13

1. *m* is the distance in miles; 2 minutes to put on gear and load the truck; the goal is *20 minutes or less*, not *less than 20 minutes*. Since 20 is a correct solution, it must be included.
2. 8 miles; 12 miles

page 21

1. $15h = 195$
2. no; 15(24) = 360, not 195
3. 13 hours; 15(13) = 195

page 22

1. 204; 1,500(204) + 14,000 = 320,000
2. $764,000

Problem Solving

1. Expressions and reasoning will vary. Example: *I used* n *to represent the number of kits. My expression is 50*n + *2*n + *10*n + *3*n + *1*n. *I used this expression instead of 66*n *so that I can identify each item included.*
2. Recommendations should include a number of kits equal to or greater than 140 and reasoning to defend the choice.
3. Answers should use the expressions and recommended number of kits to calculate how many of each item is needed.
4. Recommendations should include the number of volunteers, a number of kits equal to or less than 12 per volunteer, and an equation to prove accuracy.
5. Answers should include a number of canned goods per kit and an inequality proving that the total number of canned goods is less than or equal to 300.